GetUP

Living

Helping Yourself & Others Rise
Through Life With Purpose

Sean Crevier

ONE11

One11 Publishing
Libertyville, IL 60048

www.one11publishing.com

Publisher: Sedrik Newbern, Newbern Consulting, LLC
Editor: Linda Wolf, Network Typesetting, Inc.
Cover Designer: Scott Ventura, Integraphix, Inc.

Printed in the United States of America
First Edition: November 2018

Author's Note
This book, based on my life experiences, is for learning and teaching purposes only.

ISBN Paperback 978-1-7329512-0-4
ISBN Digital 978-1-7329512-1-1

Library of Congress Control Number: 2018962431

One11 Publishing is an imprint of
Newbern Consulting, LLC.

Dedication

For

James

Mike

Adam

I miss you!

Contents

Acknowledgments i

Intro vii

Pre-Game / Warm-Ups..1

Chapter 1: The Haiti Story 3

Chapter 2: The Early Exit..6

Chapter 3: Life In Beta 10

First Half / Act 1 14

CHAPTER 4: What Would You Do If...? 15

CHAPTER 5: 16 vs. 1 19

Chapter 6: Swear Words..24

Chapter 7: The Half-Court Shot 27

Half Time..31

Second Half / Act 2 35

Chapter 8: 6 or ½ Dozen? 37

Chapter 9: Help Me Help You...............................43

Chapter 10: Hello Ground, My Old Friend.......47

Chapter 11: Hating Happy 51

Chapter 12: Crevier... C-R-E-V-I-E-R... 9/29/39 54

Overtime / Encore 60

Chapter 13: No-Snooze Challenge 63

Chapter 14: One More Time 66

Chapter 15: Do It The Hard Way 69

Post-Game / After Party..72

About the Author..73

Acknowledgments

Sedrik

You gave me this opportunity to write this book and spread this message. But more importantly, you took away my anxiety about writing a book and let me just deliver a message. Without your confidence in me from the start, I cannot imagine having taken the leap to write something like this. Your encouragement and guidance have truly been a blessing to anyone who needs to hear the #GetUp message.

My Students & Players

For allowing me to have a career that is almost always fun and rarely work, thank you. In 20 years of teaching and coaching, you guys have always given me fantastic hope for our future. With so much negativity about "kids these days," I'm assured all the time by you that we're going to be just fine. This book had all of you at the forefront of my mind as I wrote. Your well-being kept me going during my 1 a.m. writing sessions. Because in the end, I want nothing more for you than to live an adult life with the ability to #GetUp no matter how bad it gets.

My Friends

There is a saying that "You are who you surround yourself with." This is total crap. There's no way I'm that amazing. With y'all as my group of friends, I'm definitely the smallest house in the neighborhood, constantly having my value pulled up by you. The way you guys #GetUp inspires me to keep pushing forward and provides me with constant examples that fuel my ability to spread the #GetUp message. Your friendship allows me to know that no matter how bad it gets, you've got my back.

I want to especially thank Ryan, who gave me the opportunity to give a TED talk on this topic and help spread the #GetUp message to a bigger audience. Without this opportunity, I would never have had the chance to write this book.

I also want to give special group hugs and kisses to my high school homies (Bunker, Chris, Chris, Curt, Jeff, Kev, Pete). People say we make our best friends in college—not me. My besties came into my life early and I haven't been able to get rid of them since. They were with me through a thousand ups and downs and still are. When you have friends like this, you get to live a life of giving zero shits about what anyone else thinks about you. That freedom is priceless. Without it, I have no idea who I would be right now and there's no way I would have had the courage to write this book.

Mom

I don't believe in luck, unless we talk about the lotto and I hit the parent lotto. Mom, you've always been there for me in good and bad. And even in the bad, you've cheered for me like I had a 30-point lead. As my biggest cheerleader, I've always felt like I could try anything because even if I got my ass kicked, you'd celebrate like I won the championship.

This book has been a terrifying endeavor at times. I have, on countless occasions, stopped writing mid-sentence with anxiety about "what if NOBODY buys this thing?" But then I remember that you're going to buy plenty to keep everyone involved in the black because you are you. Thank you for being you!

M&M

You two are unreal. You are my favorite students on earth.

I've always dreaded talking to you about this topic. One of the reasons I decided to take the leap and write this book is because I know that it will help you understand how serious your life is and how important it is to me that you value it with everything you have. You have no idea how much the world needs you, and you may never fully know. But please keep this book with you wherever you may go in this world. And if you run across someone who needs it more than you, give it to them and I'll get you another one. I know the guy who wrote it.

Thank you for coming into my life. I love you both so much, no matter what!

My Wife

Whew, Car! You are not only insanely supportive of #GetUp Living, but embody it. You've taught me so many ways to live it. Watching you #GetUp since the day I met you and knowing that our children get to do the same is one of my favorite things about you.

You said yes, without hesitation, to my wonky idea to start the Twitter account. You had immediate excitement the day I told you about the chance to give the TED talk. And when I brought up this book, you listened intently then immediately said you'd do whatever I needed for me to write this. I don't take for granted all the times you were my designated driver so I could write during car rides, across town, or out of town.

Not only did you give me unconditional support for writing this book, but you shot down every silly negative "what if" I threw out there as I tried talking myself out of doing this. You keep me going every day.

Thank you for all of you. I love you!

Dad

You know.

Thank you.

I love you.

I miss you.

Intro

Hi! Holy smokes, I'm super excited for you to be reading this. I, in no way, am perfect. And, if this book is 100% effective for you—well, you still won't become perfect either. Ugh, I'm so sorry. We all have insanely unique lives and there is no cookie cutter magic pill to perfect us. But we can all strengthen our current selves by exercising our minds, just like all the other muscles in our body. And #GetUp Living will give you an infrastructure under which I've found success and I believe you can too. #GetUp Living is a way to operate (or help someone else operate) to mindfully exercise the brain and strengthen its resolve to more often and more definitively overcome the daily gravity that pushes us down. It gives us that mental strength we need to harness our amazingness that the world around us so desperately needs. We were put here for a reason and I believe that we're all here for the same reason—the world needs us. So, I'd like to share it with you in case it helps you or a friend of yours or a family member or a child that you care about.

I believe that life without competition is not life. I grew up, like many kids, competing. Competing in the neighborhood with other kids, competing on sports teams, competing in the performing arts, and competing in the classroom. Competition is an amazing thing that brings so many highs and lows. The victory fist pumps bring chills that could ice down a case of beer in seconds while the salt from the tears of falling short stings so much as it runs into the scrapes and cuts from the battle. For whatever reason, I've always lived my life cycles (short, long, and every time frame in between) in terms of sports and performing arts. Everything is chunked into periods of time, whether it's my 30-minute commute to work each morning, my four years of undergrad, or my own birth to death (I think I'm at half-time but only the Big Man upstairs knows that one).

As I sit here on this airplane reflecting on my preparation process to write this book, it reminds me of my man Abe Lincoln's quote "If I were given 10 hours to cut down a tree, I'd spend the first 7 sharpening my axe." It's surreal to think that anyone might buy a ticket to this word-filled event. So, if you are reading this, thank you. Whether you paid for it yourself or you're mooching it off a family member like a shared Netflix account, thank you. Thank you for caring enough about yourself, or a friend or a family member or all of the above, to take time out to sit down in your seat (with a Chicago dog & a Coors Lite for me, please) and absorb my thoughts and philosophy on living a life with purpose, through a committed focus on **rising from falls** so that we can all become more able to #GetUp!

Pre-Game / Warm-Ups

I always loved getting to baseball games early to watch batting practice. My dad would take me to Cubs (and other teams, but mainly Cubs) games growing up and I would predictably bug him to get down there early. Standing along the brick wall at Wrigley and watching guys like Ryne Sandberg, Ron Cey, Shawon Dunston, and Jody Davis at batting practice and taking ground balls was the world's greatest appetizer. I have no idea why I enjoyed this so much, because as a kid, I was never one who loved or appreciated the pre-game in my own endeavors. I always just wanted to start the damn game. But for some reason, man, I loved getting to professional games early to watch warm-ups. There was nothing like walking down the steps in the old Chicago Stadium to watch Jordan shoot around. And when it came to musicals, the chaotic sounds of the orchestra pit warming up, like what you might hear at a zoo if every animal got food poisoning at once, were somehow soothing to my ears. I loved seeing what it took to "get things going."

All of this stuff still makes me smile and gives me the warm and fuzzy feelings inside. My dad was never real keen on getting to these events super early and I never knew why. But now, as a father, I get it. Those outings are exhausting for parents. As the adult in charge, adding extra hours onto the round-trip time is not something I love, which makes me appreciate my parents for all the times they said yes to my persistent (some may have even called it whiny) requests to get there early enough for warm-ups. So, as you open the doors and walk into this stadium of #GetUp Living, let's get warmed up a little bit. Let's stretch the hammies, throw the ball around, and loosen up the vocal cords so you can understand a little bit about why I believe so strongly in playing this game of life with such a narrowed focus on one thing—strengthening the human ability to #GetUp.

Chapter 1: The Haiti Story

At 19 years old, I was standing with my hands in the air wearing cargo shorts and a T-shirt in a gravel parking lot, with a bottle of Coke and a bag of chips dropped on the ground next to me. My eyes were locked on three men in front of me with their fingers on triggers, guns pointed, screaming at me in Creole (I don't speak Creole) in the middle of Haiti.

When I was a sophomore in undergrad, I went to Haiti on a mission trip with a campus youth group. At that time, the last thing my mom wanted me to do was to go to Haiti. I told her not to worry—"I'll be fine."

On the very first day there, our group stopped at a convenience store on our way out of the capital city, Port-A-Prince, to grab a snack for the ride. I was quick and started to head outside for fresh air to wait until the rest of the group came out. Our guide and translator told me I shouldn't go out there by myself, but since I knew everything, I told him, "I'll be fine" and went out anyway. So, as I stood there in that gravel lot, with my hands up, being screamed at and held up, I remember thinking "I'll be fine."

As the screaming and gun-pointing went on, the men walked closer, the yelling became more aggravated, and the guns started shaking vigorously. I again thought to myself, "I'll be fine." So I opened my mouth and said, in the only Creole I knew, "I don't speak Creole, I'm American." For some reason, my dumb ass thought this would resolve everything. It did not go over how I thought it would.

The three men became even more upset at that point and the guy the middle came even closer, closing in at about 5 feet. At that point, he used his gun to point down to the ground, signaling me to get onto my knees. And then, finally then, it got through my thick skull that I may not actually be fine. So I slowly dropped down, one knee at a time. As my second knee settled into the gravel, I noticed a change in tone with their faces and their voices.

All of a sudden I heard a voice behind me. Our translator had come out of the convenience store and began to explain who we were and why we were there. As they listened and calmed down, the guy closest to me, still irritated, put his foot to my chest and sent me backwards onto the gravel before turning away. Then they jumped into their truck and took off.

Haiti changed me in a lot of ways. A significant impact was the way it turned a 19-year-old kid, who always thought he'd be fine and didn't need anybody, into an adult who valued the help of other people. It wasn't just my encounter on Day

One that did this, but that certainly lit the flame for the next nine days of becoming a new person.

Without thinking about it, I returned to the States as someone who understood the need for help. One of my dad's favorite sayings was "If you want it done right, do it yourself." I still believe that there's a lot of truth in that statement. But I've learned that asking for help, while doing it myself, is nothing to be ashamed of.

We are on this Earth not for ourselves, but for each other. When things get hard, we don't have to struggle through them alone. When loved ones are in pain, it is up to us to find ways to get them to accept our help; not to enable, but to help. Being "tough" is often misconstrued as going at it alone. But real toughness is knowing when we can't do it alone and asking for help.

Haiti was the catalyst for my transformation into someone who is able to know my limits and ask for help. I'm still not perfect, but I'm a hell of a lot better than I was 24 years ago. #GetUp living is about getting up when life brings you to your knees. It's not about being a "tough guy" and always doing it yourself. It's about finding a way to the other side, even if that means asking someone else to help us #GetUp.

Chapter 2: The Early Exit

I'm an only child, please don't hold that against me. As an only child, I absolutely rocked the "imaginary friend" world. We did the most amazing things together. We were the best at everything we did. When I got old enough to trade in my imaginary friend for reality, I embraced real friendship. I immediately valued friendship, and still do, to a level that is probably one of my greatest faults. I'm picky about who I spend time with, who I trust, who I lean on.

By the time I was 35 years old, I had gone to three funerals for friends who'd committed suicide. I think about those three guys all the time. I think about what they were going through, what they were thinking, and every time I think about them, I know that I'll never know. But I am confident that they were not fine and that they didn't know what else to do.

Though I think about them a lot, I know there's nothing I can do for them anymore. But I think about my friends who struggle, my family who struggles, my students who struggle and fail and don't know what to do. And every time I think about this topic, there are two recurring emotions—sadness and anger.

One evening in December of 2011, I was thinking about my late friends and suicide and everything that comes with it. And that night, I realized I really had two options. I could go on being mad and sad or I could #GetUp and do something about it. Option One was very attractive to me, but I went with Option Two. I wanted to do something about it in a way that could help more than just my friends, my family, or my students. So, I took to Twitter—not to tell everybody what I had for breakfast that day, but to leverage its power.

I created #GetUp Living as an account to channel motivational thoughts through tweets on how to deal with struggles and failure. I wanted to provide tips and tools for what to do and how to bounce back from getting knocked down. I went this route so that anybody, not just people in my immediate world, could have the opportunity for regular exposure to tools for a lifestyle that builds grit and brings purpose into our days.

I never cared about how many followers I got. For me, it's not about building followers. It's about building a resource. For me, if just one person can benefit from it, then I'm doing something positive instead of sitting around on cold December evenings beating myself up over my friends choosing to exit this life early.

In the fall of 2015, I had an opportunity to spread the #GetUp message even more through a TED Talk. It's viewable on YouTube (just search my name and it will pop up), and I'm truly honored to have been able share #GetUp with the TED world. Like the Twitter account, if it can help just one person or help just one person help another person, then it's a success to me.

The #GetUp lifestyle continues today as you read this because of a December 2017 meeting I had about this book. This is my first book ever and hopefully not my last. Although you are reading this early in the book, it's the last chapter I'm writing. Why, right? Because I was terrified to write this chapter. I knew it was going to drain me emotionally, and I kept putting it off. But here it is.

All three stages of spreading the #GetUp message have been scary in their own way. I worried about nobody following me on Twitter. I wondered, "What if nobody watches my TED talk?" Or worse, "What if people do watch it and leave comments ripping it apart?" And with this book, as I type, my stomach is filled with nerves about it going unread by anyone other than my family and publisher.

With all three steps I've taken to share the #GetUp life, I've gone through the yes/no back-and-forth shuffle before actually getting up and doing it. It's scary. But the reason I said "yes" in the end with all three is because I'm a member of the Lucky Sperm Club. I don't believe much in luck, but the family in which we are born is all luck. To no credit of my own, I was born into a life where my parents and other adults taught and prepared me to be able to bounce back from failure. Without that preparation, there is no way I would have had the confidence to create the Twitter account, give the TED Talk, or write this book. Spreading the #GetUp lifestyle is my way of sharing my luck and trying to help others benefit from my fortunate upbringing.

There is such a strong culture in our world today that attempts to convince kids to push themselves to go beyond their comfort zones. I absolutely love the intention, but I have a problem with the execution because I hate the action of convincing. When we convince someone to do something, we may be forcing them into a situation for which they are not prepared.

Instead of convincing kids to push themselves to go further than they've ever gone before, we must face the reality that they may not actually be able to go that far yet. And if they did, are they equipped to handle it? Convincing is great if they don't fail—but what if they do? We need to equip kids to take risks so if it doesn't go their way, they have a plan. Equipping kids to take risks begins with equipping them to #GetUp.

Chapter 3: Life In Beta

Google has figured a LOT of things out over the last 15–20 years. When they launched Gmail in 2004, they launched it in beta status. In the software world, putting something out to the public while it was still in beta was not the norm. But Google kept Gmail in beta for over five years. Although it was an email product with a continuously compounding adoption rate, Google's "beta" stamp sent a clear message that was bigger than email or software or technology. The extended beta status, while available for public consumption, said, "We're not perfect." Those are such empowering words!

Google is NOT perfect because Google is just simply a compilation of a bunch of humans. The human brain is the computer for our body through which we run software. Emotional and rational software are constantly running and developing throughout our lives. Although the brain stops developing physically as we elevate into adulthood, the operating system is always changing. It's so important for both the emotional and rational apps running our brains to continue to grow, improve, and upgrade. Recognizing that is not typically a challenge for us humans. The hard part, the humbling part, is the default that comes with this recognition. Every decision to do something is, by default, paired (often less obviously) with another decision to not do something else. In my world of teaching accounting and economics, we call the latter an opportunity cost. So by saying, "Yes! Of course, we must continuously upgrade the software in our brain." We are also saying, "Nope, our brains will never reach a point of perfection." That's a tough sentence to live out because in order to be true to it, we have to be okay with screwing up and accepting that we'll always be dealing with bugs in our system.

I've been playing organized sports since I was four and coaching them for 19 years. One of the most challenging hang-ups for athletes happens during the pre-game warm-ups. As a spectator, you already know that I love warm-ups. As a coach and player, I absolutely hate them. They are so necessary for our body and I'd never skip them, but they are a mental grind. The real goal of warm-ups is to get the blood flowing, the muscle memory triggered, and the body loosened up. Unfortunately, for so many, it becomes a last-minute practice, like cramming for a final exam at 2 a.m. the night before or day of. Like taking a final exam, when it's game day, if you don't know it by now, then you don't know it. But players get mental (myself included) and want to make sure they're hitting the perfect shots on the range before they head to the first tee. I've had hundreds of rounds of golf where I was a machine on the driving range and then went out and played like absolute trash. Conversely, I've had the same number of times where I stunk it up on the range yet still killed it out on the course. Putting a hard limit on how many balls you hit, how many three-point shots you take, how many pitches you throw before taking the field is essential. We can't wait until we get it perfect to go start. The process is the key, not the results. We've gotta trust the process and know that we're not going to achieve perfection every time. We are "in beta" constantly and when we commit to that, the potential for growth goes through the roof because we start embracing failure as a chance to upgrade.

The amazing Amy Poehler said, *"Great people do things before they're ready. They do things before they know they can do it. Doing what you're afraid of, getting out of your comfort zone, taking risks like that—that is what life is. You might be really good. You might find out something about yourself that's really special and if you're not good, who cares? You tried something. Now you know something about yourself."*

So, next game/match/round/big meeting/huge speech that you get to play a part in, stay in beta. Remember that no warm-up will be perfect, no driving-range session will ever send us to the first tee feeling like we're gonna go under par today. So we just have to get as ready as we can each day, put the pads on, and tee the ball up, because it's time for kickoff—"ready" or not.

Life in beta is an entire life of learning about ourselves and doing something about the bugs. Sean 42.6 is writing this book right now with things that he's learned so far. By no means am I perfect or claiming that this will make you perfect. But I'm better than before and I believe that this will help you make yourself or a loved one better by accepting the next bug as a chance to #GetUp.

First Half / Act 1

The emotions involved with trying to harness the natural energy created when the race gun goes off are insane. Starting the event, when those curtains open, looking around at everyone watching in the audience, the stands, the sidelines... whew! Holy crap!

The first half of an event opens so strong. I love the way rock stars come out onto the stage to open their concerts. Music has always been an integral part of my life. My first concert ever was, wait for it... Michael Jackson. Yup! When I was 10, my dad took me to Comiskey Park for a colossal musical performance experience that I'll never top, ever. I peaked at 10! My concert-going career opened with the King (Sorry LeBron, you ain't got nothin' on him) of Pop.

Filled with human fuel when we're young in anything, whether it's life, a new job, a new hobby, even starting to write your first book, feels amazing. And then, inevitably, still with a full tank, the reality that we have a long-ass way to go gives us a first-round Mike Tyson jab to the face. And then we realize the need to settle in because we know that no human can sustain that level of excitement or energy for the long haul. So we find a reasonable pace, not necessarily comfortable, but reasonable, and settle in.

CHAPTER 4: What Would You Do If...?

I love the current momentum in society for people to push, explore, and attempt without reservation. "Innovation" is such a big buzzword right now. As much as I hate buzzwords ("circle back" is my current front runner for giving me the biggest visceral reaction), innovation and the push for it is so fantastic. A "go-to" question that I've been seeing all too often over the past few years is "What would you do if you knew you couldn't fail?" Ugh! If you love that, please trust me and do me a favor... stop, just stop right now.

What holds us back from pushing, exploring, and attempting things that may be at the edge of (or even further beyond) our perceived capability is the post-failure picture. If I ask anyone with a brain to "pretend" that they could not fail, it will NOT address the real source of apprehension. We all know that there's a chance of falling short with everything we do.

When my son was in 1st grade, he came home one day and there was clearly something going on in his head. I went right into "dad mode" and asked the standard afterschool question... "Hey Bubba, how was your day?" I was ready to keep doing what I was doing because I fully expected the programmed answer of "Fine" to come back at me. Instead, he got teary-eyed, looked right at me, and said, "Not good, Dad." I was so happy!! Not because he had a bad day, but because he opened that door to talk about it. So, I asked him what happened and he proceeded to tell me about a colossal milk-spilling incident at lunch that day. All the kids (1st-grade boys) at his table erupted in laughter and began to make fun of him. Pretty standard response. And to be honest, I kinda laughed a bit while he was telling me the story.

I'm a fixer and I had his attention. This was right in my wheelhouse and I was pumped thinking, "I got this!" My mind was racing with strategies for how he could set himself up to not spill his milk again. Luckily, before speaking, I bought a few seconds with a big hug. During that hug, I thought about proper milk placement within his given eating area. I considered teaching him how to open his milk only slightly so that if it did tip, it wouldn't spill as much. So many logistical ideas came to mind for milk-spill prevention that I could turn it into a retirement career. As the hug finished and I looked him in those teary eyes, it hit me that he got his klutziness from his mother and he will FOR SURE be spilling something at lunch again, no matter how great these new strategies might be. His sadness wasn't from the milk, or the spill, or anything that caused the kids to laugh at him. It was simply that the kids were laughing at him.

So, I scrapped it all and instead of working towards preventing failure, instead of asking him to pretend like he'll never spill again, we talked about what to do if (more likely WHEN) it happens again. It was extremely difficult for me to pass on fixing the spill situation; I really think I had some solid ideas. So, I asked him, "Do you think that if you spill again, they'll laugh again?" "For sure, Dad." "Could you convince them to not laugh at you, or to stop?" "Dad!"

(Now, I know those boys very well. I absolutely love that class of boys. They are a fierce, competitive, relentless, nonstop, loud-as-all-get-out, amazing class of boys. I've had the pleasure of coaching them. They crack me up, they drive me bonkers, they fight against each other to win at recess, but best of all is that when push comes to shove, they've got each other's backs in the end. Watching them fight together to win is something everyone should get to experience. If you're into middle school basketball, hit me up on Twitter and I'll give you their schedule. It's a treat.)

I knew he would answer the way he did to those questions, but I needed the answers to those questions to be at the forefront of his brain before we moved on. So I said, "Alright, dude. If that's the case, then you've got a really solid option." Still sad and slightly mad, he said with massive doubt and impressive eye-rolling, "Like what?" I said, "You've gotta laugh with them. Listen, you have to admit, what you did is kinda funny. It even made me laugh a little when you told me about it. So, if you don't want them to laugh AT you, then start laughing. If you're laughing too, now they're laughing WITH you instead of laughing AT you." Problem solved! I could see the gears turning in his head as his face evolved into a little smile. Now, luckily, in addition to the klutziness, my son also got my wife's smile which is contagiously heartwarming. To have the smile back painted on that face was the absolute best. He was good to go and I knew he was done with this. I said, "How was the rest of your day?" He said, "Fine."

Trying to get people to pretend like they'll never fail is insane to me. It's insane to anyone with half a brain because we all know that there's always a risk of the bottom falling out. We can prepare all we want. We can minimize risk and carry a rabbit's foot in our pocket. But the realists know that we can still fail. So, instead, let's ask ourselves or our loved ones, adults or kids, "What would you do if you knew that you could deal with the failure?" Let's help people deal with failure instead of build false hope. Preparing for the worst and working toward the best is what keeps people innovating, pushing, grinding. Let's build ourselves, our friends, and our children up so that they take risks because they know that if they fail, they'll be able to #GetUp!

CHAPTER 5: 16 vs. 1

Why the heck does everybody love the underdog? The bigger the underdog, the more beloved you are. March basketball is one of the greatest times of year. The 16 seed versus the 1 seed, 15 vs. 2, 14 vs. 3, oh man, so great!! At the time of writing this, only one 16 seed has EVER beat a 1 seed in the Men's NCAA basketball tournament, and that just happened this past year. Previous to this past year, it had NEVER happened, ever! So, why even play the game? We all "know" who's gonna win, right? Just call it done and save everyone the time, sweat, money, tears, bruises, and everything else that comes along with a battle!

Being an underdog is a right of passage in life. If you've never been a true underdog, go find a way to be one. Get out there, give it a go—like a for-real go, not some half-assed token effort just to say you did it. Really, truly go try to win something that you have NO business even thinking about winning.

Life is hard, super hard, for everyone. We are all underdogs in the game of life. It constantly throws bombs at us, sometimes anticipated but often completely out of the blue. One of my best friends jokes (but not totally) about today's generation and their inability to deal with the surprising BS that life throws at us. He blames it on the extinction of the "Jack-in-the-Box." If you're old enough to have played with one, you probably just experienced a little anxiety thinking about turning that crank and listening to the terrifying song that plays until that creepy little clown dude pops up and makes you pee yourself just a little... EVERY. SINGLE. TIME.

Life isn't supposed to be easy. It's convenient to look at someone and think, "Boy, they've sure got it easy." I'm sure we all know someone in our lives who we've thought that about. But really, they've got some shit going on, too. We may not know about it, but it's there, and they wake up every day knowing that it's there. Some days they spend more time battling it and some days are less demanding. But when we grab a 360 look at the world around us, every living human we see has life stacked up against them. If we can accept this and help our loved ones accept this, then we get to join the club of underdogs and play the game.

Playing the game as an underdog is not always fun and often has some pretty crappy stuff happen. But I've never seen a 16 seed pull a no-show. They play because there's still fun in the process. Win or lose, it's worth it to give it a go, just in case.

I consider myself extremely fortunate (that's a choice, by the way) in several areas of my life. One of those areas that I love is how my motivation source has evolved. When I was little, the "you can do this" from my parents was all I needed. In my late teens, those encouraging words and back pats began to do nothing for me. I experienced a shift as a person and was fortunate enough to become motivated by doubters. Now, at 42, if you tell me that I've got this, that's super nice of you. However, it's going to do absolutely nothing for me. Look me in the eyes and tell me I'm nuts and you've all but sealed the deal. I thrive on the naysayers; I actually seek them out at this point because I know they hold my fuel.

When I was 24, I blew out my ACL (and the entire rest of my knee) because I thought I was still 18 and played a pick-up basketball game as if I was 15. Half way through the game I had a fast break (that's relative because I'm slow as all get out) and there was a defender right on my tail. I knew that if I went right up with it, that ball would get swatted out of the gym from behind. So, I jump-stopped to let him go by and my right knee spun around faster than a Tilt-a-Whirl at the county fair.

After surgery, rehab was a bear. My physical therapist was awesome and pushed me like crazy. However, she also changed my life one day with her words. I asked her if I was going to be able to be ready to play softball this upcoming season with my old-man softball team. She said, "We'll for sure have you ready to play softball. But you'll never be able to run long distances again." I laughed and said, "What do you mean?" She said, "Well, you did a real job on that knee. So, long-distance running wear and tear is not something your knee will be able to handle. But softball is fine."

What she didn't realize is that I had never run more than 2 miles straight in my entire life. I was a golfer and baseball player growing up. Running was never really something that I did much of. But, on that day, she really ticked me off telling me that I couldn't do something. So, a year later I ran a 5k and now, at 42, I do multiple triathlons a year (not Iron Man competitions; I'm not that insane) and always have some kind of race lined up to conquer in the near future.

I don't think we should stop encouraging kids or stop enjoying encouragement. However, one of the toughest parts of life is when you feel like nobody is on your team. It's incredibly easy to feel like the entire world is against us, hatin' on every move we make. If we can help our loved ones embrace being the underdog, we can minimize the negative impact of haters and harness that hate into energy and power to overcome. As wonderful as it would be for anti-bullying campaigns to have 100% success, that's just not going to happen. Let's not lead our kids to think that it will. I don't think we should scrap those campaigns, but we MUST prepare ourselves and our youth so that they have the skills to fight the uphill battle. If we can do that, then no matter how tough it gets, we are still able to lace up the shoes and #GetUp!

Chapter 6: Swear Words

Being a parent is crazy difficult. I have no idea how I'm doing it. My children are 8 and 11 and the last 11 years has been one big blur. My wife is a saint and really the rock-solid foundation that keeps our children alive and well. Our kids are pretty normal, active kids. They play baseball, are in band, take dance lessons, do after school art club, etc. We run our household like a team and Team Crev has a strict no-swearing policy. However, our swear words are not the typical list of swear words you'd see in a list. Our swear words are excuse-making words that today's society seems to love using. These words, when accepted by others, are the same as participation trophies, rewarding someone for something they didn't do. All of them reference action but don't include any action. Here's the Big 3 Team Crev swear word list:

Try
Hope
'Ould

Try: Tom Hanks made it very clear to the world that, "There's no crying in baseball!" In our house, there's no trying on Team Crev. The ease with which I hear kids fall back on "I tried" is nauseating and worse than that is when an adult lets a kid off the hook with "It's okay, you tried."

That word is extremely empty, but unfortunately very accepted and widely used. I used to work with a teacher who challenged kids whenever they said they were going to "try harder" next time. She would ask them, "What does that look like?" I've learned, through that approach, that kids have no idea what that entails, which means they have no clue what the word "try" truly means. On Team Crev, we replace "tried" with what we actually did that resulted in failure. When we do this, it means a lot more and has a built-in reflection component which is essential for growth and improvement.

Hope: Hope is what you do before you open a present and there is only one thing you want it to be, so you "hope" it's that. Hoping does nothing to make things happen. Whenever my kids truly want something to happen, they don't get to hope for it. They know they have the power to increase the likelihood of getting it, but that power requires thoughtful and intentional action, not hoping. I'm not saying that we shouldn't HAVE hope. There's a big difference between hope as a verb versus hope as a noun. Having hope (the noun) can be inspirational, it can keep spirits alive and help someone push through and #GetUp from hard times. As a noun it's a powerful thing. However, as a verb it is a very dangerous word. Hoping (verb) can actually damage having real hope (noun) because there's a sense of emptiness created when there is no action. So instead of hoping, on Team Crev we act intentionally, and hoping is not an act.

'Ould: One of my dad's favorite Dad-isms was "Woulda coulda shoulda shit!" *Would* and *could* and *should* are three of the most evil words in the English language. They give us an out and place a "maybe" on past, present, and future action. To #GetUp, there must be action. That action can be slow, slight, gradually building to the point where you may not even be able to spot it. But, there has to be some sort of action. The power of committing, 100%, to action is extremely underrated. The evil 'oulds prevent full commitment and immediately decrease any likelihood of action. Team Crev talks about what we did, are doing, and will do—not about what we woulda, coulda, or shoulda done.

To get living the #GetUp life, action is key, no matter how small the action may be. Taking a small action step like eliminating a few toxic words from your vocabulary can be the perfect spark for your life. Getting rid of this action-killing vocab will help you or your loved ones navigate a life more focused on the #GetUp.

Chapter 7: The Half-Court Shot

I've always wanted to be the dude who got to go down to center court at halftime of a pro or college game and launch a half-court shot to win a car. Not a chance do I think I'd make it, but man, would I love to give it a go. I'd love to find out how I would react in that situation. Feeling what it's like to have tens of thousands of people watching and cheering me on would be amazing. There's just something about the half-court shot. When I coach my son's basketball team, all the boys want to do is launch half-court shots and honestly, I do too. We all want to be the hero to hit the one-handed baseball throw buzzer beater or use all our might to throw the 70-yard Hail Mary (Aaron Rodgers style) to win the game with no time left on the clock.

Attempting the "impossible" is something we humans are enthralled with. It goes back to that notion of being the underdog—little David and his slingshot against the giant. We are somehow so attracted to the "but what if" piece of it that we ignore all potential fear of failing because it's so easy to #GetUp from that failure. It's the same "but what if" that drives us to throw our money away playing the lottery. There's a giddiness about this insane potential scenario that consumes us. Several years ago, I was coming home from a golf trip to Michigan (if you play golf and haven't played in southwest Michigan, do it) with a bunch of buddies. The Lotto jackpot had built up to some incredibly high amount and we all bought tickets on our way out of town. The entire 2-hour drive home was spent talking about what we'd do if we won. We postulated about everything imaginable like, how we'd quit our jobs, how long we'd wait to tell people, the first thing we'd buy under $50,000, where we'd move, who we'd share the money with, etc. Not once did anyone ask, "But what if we don't win?"

That careless approach to playing the game, whether it be the lottery or the half-time half-court shot is so mentally freeing. Why can't we approach everything that way? Why do we get so nervous about doing some things and less nervous about others? In the end, it's all about what's on the line and how difficult it will be to #GetUp from the worst-case scenario. The more we have on the line, the more difficult it will be to #GetUp from the failure. However, the more we're able to build our #GetUp muscles, the less nervous we get about those situations. The ability to not give a damn is an essential muscle to build when living the #GetUp life. Not giving a damn isn't about not giving a damn. It's about knowing that I'll be okay in the end regardless of the outcome.

I've had the opportunity to coach some amazing kids over the past 19 years. During that time, I've also had the opportunity to have a few really,

really good teams. I'll take good kids over good athletes any day. But when you fall into a season where you have both, boy, is that a gorgeous thing. One year, my girls' golf team fit that profile. I had an amazing crew of girls who were also really good golfers. We had a chance that year to go further in the state series than a girls' golf team had ever gone at our school. We put the work in physically. We practiced and took copious notes on the course several times leading up to the tournament. We did all of the due diligence we could and paid a ton of attention to detail throughout the process.

Now it was game day and the girls were insanely nervous on the morning of the round. Coaching high school golf is really just being a psychologist who knows the rules of golf, and my stupid jokes were not loosening them up like normal, nor were any of my other typically successful coaching strategies. So we put the clubs away and went back to the bus. All the other teams were out there warming up hard-core and we went to the bus. I looked at every single one of them before I started talking and then I said, "Look, I don't give a damn how we do today." They looked at me like I was crazy. I continued, "And I need you guys to do the same." One girl said, "But we care a lot about this." I said, "I know, and I love that, and I care a lot too. But I need you to care enough to not care. You guys are caring so much right now that you're gonna care yourselves right out of this tournament."

None of this was planned, it just came out, I had nothing left in my bag of tricks, so I just talked to them honestly. I explained to them that no matter how we did, we would still go home tonight to our loving family and go to school tomorrow to teachers who care about us and our friends who make us laugh. But I guaranteed them that if they didn't stop caring so much, they would only decrease their likelihood of having success. As we broke our meeting, I made them all look at me and tell me "I don't care." It worked. We did it. Now, "Care enough not to care" is the most successful approach my teams follow when in high-pressure situations with a lot on the line.

Not giving a damn is about caring enough not to care. Working with ourselves or with our loved ones to understand that the "worst case scenario" is really not as bad as it seems lets us strut (not nervously shuffle) into that meeting and absolutely own it. Not giving a damn gives us the half-court shot mental freedom to shoot any shot knowing that regardless of the results, we absolutely WILL be able to #GetUp.

Half Time

Climb

Fall

Puke

#GetUp

Repeat

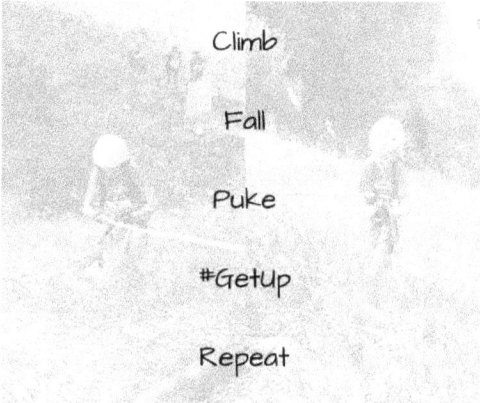

I want...
I wish...
I wonder...
Stop with all those W's!! Only 1 "W" matters.
I WILL #GetUp from...
I WILL #GetUp and...
I WILL #GetUp to...

My love of sports came from, yup, my dad. And late in the fourth quarter of his life, he was down big time. Just getting his butt kicked. Living the #GetUp life is not about always winning. It's about always believing that you can still win the next possession or the next act or the next 2 minutes, no matter what the total score may be.

GetUp
@getupliving

What's comin at you this week is comin at you...no matter what. How will you #GetUp & counter attack? #WinTheMoment

GetUp
@getupliving

When you help those you love #GetUp, your own life shines with more purpose to #GetUp for yourself.

GetUp
@getupliving

#GetUp & love more..#GetUp from the petty stuff & argue less. #GetUp & #live this only life you get here on earth!

Being "tough" is often misconstrued as going at it alone.

But real toughness is knowing when we can't #GetUp alone and ask for help.

GetUp
@getupliving

Do things that make you uncomfortable. #GetUp for challenges that you're not sure you can meet. Learn from the #journey, not the result!

GetUp
@getupliving

#Hope is great for what "could" be. #Sweat is great for what WILL be. Don't let hope replace sweat. #Getup and go work for what you want!

One of the toughest parts of
life is when you feel like nobody
is on your team.
It's incredibly easy to feel like
the entire world is against us...
#GetUp & be a team-mate for
someone.

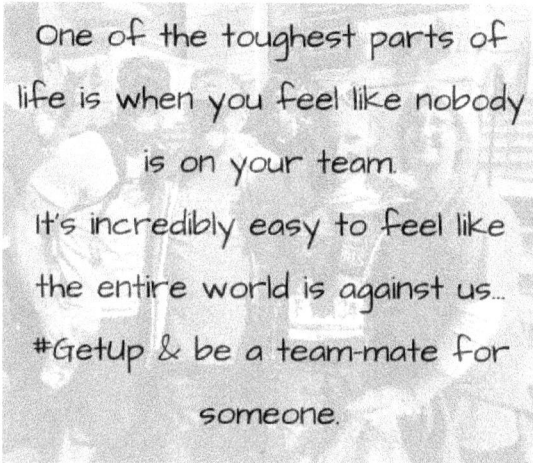

GetUp
@getupliving

When #life makes you weak,
find your strong, #GetUp &
overcome! "Strong" does not
come from what u can already
do. It comes from overcoming
the things u once thought you
could not.

GetUp
@getupliving

"What would you do if you knew
you couldn't fail" is bogus!
"What would you do if you knew
you'd #GetUp & be fine if you
do fail" is more like it! What
would you #GetUp for in #life if
you knew you'd be fine after
failing at it?

GetUp
@getupliving

3 hours of sleep w/ a body that's
a sore, hot mess... and you're
staring 7+ miles in the eye! You
don't have to know "how", you
just gotta GetUp & put
#1FootInFrontOfTheOther!
#RagnarChi @RagnarRelay

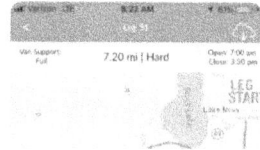

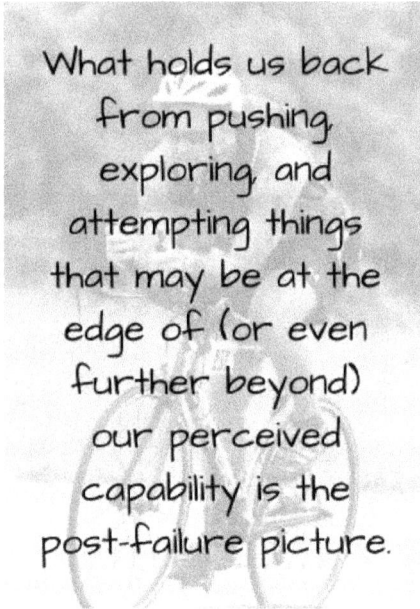

What holds us back from pushing, exploring, and attempting things that may be at the edge of (or even further beyond) our perceived capability is the post-failure picture.

GetUp
@getupliving

Sometimes you just gotta #GetUp & go... especially when conditions suck!

GetUp
@getupliving

#RaceDay #GetUp

GetUp
@getupliving

You are who you surround yourself with. #GetUp & love the good people in your life to become a tribe of awesomeness!

Second Half / Act 2

As we begin the second half of anything, we have renewed energy. If we're competing or performing, we've had a chance to step back, relax, get some water, wipe the sweat, and hit a bit of an official reset button on our minds and body. If we're spectators, we've stepped out and gotten a consumable energy booster (cheese fries and another Coors Light for me, please).

The second half brings great excitement for "more" with a hint of anxiety about how it will go. If the first half was rockin', we know we need to continue the momentum into part 2 for a complete performance. But we've all had first halves that didn't go so well. In those games, we come out of the break knowing we have to focus on fundamentals and turn things around. Finding a way to create momentum we didn't really find in the first half is key. Either way, one thing that holds true is a great baseball-ism reminding us that, "Yesterday's homeruns don't win today's games." What's behind us is behind us—good, bad, or somewhere in the middle. Right now doesn't care about anything other than right now.

So, we buckle in for the plays ahead, trying to harness that renewed energy while still staying settled in to the big picture game. That mindset sends the body jitters, strength, and some flashes of limping weakness driven by the natural nervousness about what's to come. But the beauty of it is that we HAVE CONTROL of what comes. We don't have complete control of the results, but we have control over how we react to each piece of this new half as we navigate through it, remembering FDR's wisdom that, "a smooth sea never made a skilled sailor."

Chapter 8: 6 or ½ Dozen?

Growing up, not once did I ever want to be a teacher. I wanted to be a professional baseball player, and my back-up plan was the business world. When I ended up going back (after getting an undergrad degree in business) for a Master's program in secondary education, I had no clue what to expect. We had all sorts of late 90's educational philosophy thrown at us. Everyone had their own opinion (this is still so true today) on everything from seating arrangements to quality of assessment questions. And, there were enough "classroom management techniques" to fill the ocean.

One of the best things I learned in that program came from my favorite professor (I took three classes from her) who at the time was addressing the amount of content that needs to be covered during a semester class. She not only talked about it from our perspective as future teachers trying to deliver all of that content in limited time, but also from a student perspective. We walked through the student experience when they look at the syllabus for the class or even the learning objectives for a given unit. We talked a lot about helping kids navigate through overwhelming learning scenarios, like a longer-than-usual chapter of material or a busier-than-usual time of year (like college application deadline time for seniors). She told us we approach this the same way we'd approach eating an elephant—one bite at a time. That stuck with me.

I'm easily overwhelmed, I catch myself waiting to start things because I don't have time to get it all done now. But chunking, or breaking things down into digestible bites, is the only way things get done. When we, or our loved ones, feel hopeless and don't know how we're going to get through something, it's typically because we have fallen into a mindset that we have to do it all at once. When the stock market crashes, it works its way back slowly. No investor expects it regain all of its value tomorrow. When we go through a series of setbacks, or even if we take one giant roundhouse punch, we stare at this mountain ahead of us that we'll need to climb in order to #GetUp. The only way to climb that mountain is one bite at a time.

My wife has a motto that we've adopted for Team Crev—"I can do anything for one year." Don't get hung up on the time frame of 365 days. That's a variable that can and should be changed to fit the specific situation. We encountered a few scenarios early in our lives together that we needed to look at and say, "we can do this for a year." But life also throws things at us where we just need to say, "Okay, we can do this for a week." Life is a journey with checkpoints, and finding ways to make it to the next checkpoint is a key to being able to #GetUp and move on.

My favorite book of all time is "Oh, the Places You'll Go" by the great Dr. Seuss. I love it because it's all about the journey and the checkpoints and getting from one to another with happiness, struggles, and excitement. But could you imagine if that book was called "Oh, the Place You'll End Up"? That's not so fun because it's six feet underground for every single one of us. Sometimes the journey is easy and fun and whimsical as if nothing can go wrong. Other times, it's filled with darkness, sleet, wet socks with wrinkly feet, and a flashlight with a dying battery. It's the latter where we really need to tap into our ability to break our present and near future into chunks like we're eating an elephant.

Chunking is all about semantics, to give ourselves the mental approach we need to keep moving forward. Whether we break something up into six individual pieces or lump it all together as a half dozen, it doesn't matter. What does matter is finding out what type of chunking works for each of us. Maybe it's neither for you, and you prefer to move forward with two sets of three!

I'm a racer, my wife is a racer, my dad was a racer (ran track & cross country in college and the Chicago marathon at 68 years old) and we are putting our children into races. Racing is amazing, and I've never won a thing in any race. The wonder of racing comes from its full-force submersion into discovering your personal approach to chunking. I've been in a lot of races where I've enjoyed the race. I've also had a lot of races that were horrible from start to finish—I love these the most because they force me to find new ways of chunking.

I was recently in one of these horrible races with a group of friends. We decided to run Ragnar which is about a 200-mile continuous race. Someone on the team is always running and it goes on for almost two days. On my third run of the race it was midday with the sun pounding and high humidity. I'd already put decent mileage in, and I was running on no more than 2 hours of sleep that I'd gotten in the driver's seat of a parked van. I had a 7.5-mile run in front of me and I almost started to cry as I saw my teammate running toward me to pass the torch onto me to start that leg of our journey. I looked down the trail that was my exit path, looked at my legs, and had no idea how I was going to get my body to the first turn, let alone through all 7.5 miles. The only thing I knew was that there was no way in hell I was going to turn my back on this.

That run was the most challenging single run I've ever done. By mile 4, my chunking was all the way down to one step. I've never thought about the mechanics of moving my legs more in my life than during those last 3.5 miles. I just kept going. "Just get to that next shady spot up ahead and then figure it out from there." "One more step…

now one more... now one more." When I turned the corner and saw my team waiting for me, yelling, I sped up with energy I really didn't have. I felt like I was Usain Bolt in that last .1 mile (unfortunately, the video of it does not confirm that feeling). Regardless, I finished.

To race is to finish. True racers will do everything they can to avoid having "DNF" (Did Not Finish) posted next to their name in the results column. On Team Crev, we don't DNF. If you've raced, you get it. If you haven't yet, please give it a shot. Racing is not about winning against other people, it's about winning against yourself and the challenges of the world. Find a race that you're willing to give a shot, and then do it. Don't worry about it being a long distance and absolutely do not worry about time—just finish and then you, too, will get it.

I have business people come into my classroom to talk to my students quite often. One time, I had a partner at a big firm come in. My students got him onto the topic of interviewing and hiring new employees. One kid asked him what was the one thing he looked for most in a candidate. He said he loved hiring racers because they know how to finish. No matter what, he knew that he could put them on a project and it would get done.

It's not easy to be a finisher, but it is pretty simple. Whatever it is that you or your loved one are going through, take some time to chunk your challenges into digestible bites. Get to the next checkpoint and then figure out the next chunk once you're there. But in order to finish, you must first decide to start. To start, we must move one foot forward (as slowly as we need to) and then put the other foot in front of that one (maybe a tad bit faster). Don't focus on the finish—that will come as long as we chunk into bites and #GetUp.

Chapter 9: Help Me Help You

One of the greatest ways our mind misleads us when we are in a slump is with the feeling of uselessness. When we begin to question our purpose for being here on Earth, we also begin to consider an Earth without us. "They would never miss me if I'm gone" or "Things are probably better off without me anyway" are common thoughts that people have who contemplate ending their own lives early. It's human nature to question our existence. It's human nature to wonder if we are doing this "life thing" the right way. Questioning our practice, in anything, is not only natural, but it's good for us. But to think that nature doesn't need us on this Earth is tragic.

The driving forces behind peoples' desire to leave this Earth early are so very different from one to another. However, once we convince ourselves that we aren't important to anyone else, we've also justified our negative thinking and taken a huge step closer to that final fatal decision to end it.

For those of us who are religious, spiritual, or neither, in times of rational mindsets, we know that we can always bring some level of value somewhere to someone. Every major world religion carries a common belief that helping others is good for us. As a numbers person, I just can't believe that all of those religions and people are wrong about that one same thing.

As Tom Cruise's title character, Jerry McGuire, tells his one and only client, "Help me help you!" When we help other people, we bring ourselves into a different world than the one in which we normally operate. Not only does it give us a reprieve from our own life, but I believe it delivers two significant benefits that can help us avoid that feeling of uselessness and justification for creating an early departure for ourselves.

First of all, when we help others, we are investing our time in another person and their life. Any time we have a vested interest in something or someone else, we have a more natural energy level to "keep going." Part of us is now a part of them. And when we devote ourselves to something, we want to see how it plays out, and we must keep going in order to do so.

Second, when we are helping another person, we are typically much more rational than if we're trying to help ourselves. I give other people way better advice than I give myself. I've had hundreds of "aha" moments while helping someone else. I learn so much when I'm supporting someone else with their struggles. It's amazing how clear-minded we can be when we're working through someone else's challenges with them. Simply put, helping other people gives us a new perspective that we often need for our own lives.

My dad was a natural helper and teacher. Although never in a school setting, he was always teaching and showing people things. It was magical watching the way my children listened to him when he was showing them how to play chess, how to trap a squirrel, how to play blackjack, etc. It was also magical to watch him continue to help and teach, even in the last year, months, and weeks of his life. I have no clue what he went through, mentally, as he lived out his incurable battle with cancer. But I do know that he never once stopped helping others.

He and my mother were heavily involved in our church's mission group and annual trips to a sister parish in Peru for 14 years prior to his passing away. He was always in charge of communications between US and Peru families, which included being the email middleman for digital photo-sharing. Toward the end of his battle, his medications had taken such a toll on him that he no longer had feeling in any of his fingertips. One day, just a couple months before we lost him, I was at my parents' house. I walked into his office and he was on the computer, working. But I noticed that he had taped his right hand to the mouse and he was typing with only his left. He looked physically miserable. I knew the tape job was because the neuropathy in his hands had become so severe that he couldn't properly manipulate the mouse in a normal way. It took all I had not to break down in tears. With a quiver in my voice, I said, "Dad, why don't you let someone else take that job over for you?" He said with full conviction, "Because I want to do it."

Duh!

I had completely ignored his mental needs. I was so focused on what he needed physically that I became blind to his need for purpose. What I hadn't considered was that even though he was physically miserable, he was mentally where he wanted and needed to be. He was helping others. He was continuing to be useful while still on this Earth.

When we help other people, we simultaneously help ourselves with whatever has us down. If you're down, help someone else. If a friend or a loved one is down, help them help someone else, and maybe that someone else can be you. Something as simple as, "I need your help" can go a long way for a friend who is down. I think the natural move with any friend who is down is to ask how we can help them. But often when we are in a slump, we don't care about ourselves enough to accept help. And in that case, asking them to help us is the best way to help them. If you help someone help you, you'll help them #GetUp.

Chapter 10: Hello Ground, My Old Friend

It's amazing to me how the timing of things works. Think about the last time you were looking to buy a new car and you decided which type of car you wanted next. Now, over the course of the next several days, how many times did you see that car on the road? All over the place, right? Crazy! Whether it's coincidental, or heightened awareness, or the universe messing with us, it happens in so many scenarios.

I've known that I was going to write this chapter today for about a week. And holy smokes, what a week it has been. We (Team Crev) have spent a lot of time with our friend, the ground, over the last six days. I won't get into the details, but my daughter had an emergency procedure on her mouth, my son went through an emotional tryout process that didn't end well, I was denied a position in a confidence-shattering way, and my wife had little to no sleep several nights in a row as our household rock trying to manage all three scenarios like the champ she is.

I believe that the Big Man upstairs is very intentional about putting things in our lives at certain times. I think this chapter being in the forefront of my mind was the guiding light that allowed me to help all of us get through the last seven days. If you look at our @GetUpLiving Twitter account and check out the tweet from 8/8/18, you'll see a message from The Rock that showed up in my feed exactly when my son and I needed to see it.

The Rock is in Vancouver Canada. His message is about how important that city is to him, his life path, and where he is now in his career. At 22 years old, he came to Vancouver to play his first Canadian Football League game while playing for the Calgary Stampeders. He was so excited that day to be playing in the first CFL game of his career. Two days later, he got cut and sent home with dreams shattered. He couldn't believe it, because his big dream was to eventually play in the NFL. But he quickly says that he realized that playing in the NFL was the best thing that never happened to him because it allowed him to get to where he is now.

It's so easy to look at people, super-famous or locally known, and resent them for being "lucky" and having "overnight success." But unless they are a lottery winner, nobody really is an overnight success. The successful have been knocked down just as many times as the unsuccessful. The difference between the two is how you greet the ground when you land face-first.

Winners and succeeders hit the ground and embrace Momma Earth. They say hello with an unhappy but comfortable familiarity that says "Here we go again" with a smile. Winners know that they can't always win. Winners use the ground as a place to reset, reflect, rest a bit, and re-energize. But they always #GetUp and go back at it.

When we hit the ground, we often feel like we're out of gas and it's easy for us to resent the ground and its dirtiness. But if we embrace the ground the way winners do, we appreciate it for keeping us from falling further. If we embrace the ground the way winners do, we kiss it hello and goodbye at the same time. Whatever scrapes and bruises are created in our fall, we "rub some dirt on it" and #GetUp for our next adventure.

In these past seven days of the Team Crev struggle, my kids (8 and 11 years old) ran a 1.5 – 2 hour adventure race. In a 5k distance, they completed 15 physically demanding challenges in brutal Midwest summer 90-degree heat with insane humidity. My 11-year-old son had a fever that morning and decided to run the race anyway. After 45 minutes into the race and having just completed the 8th challenge, climbing up a super-steep hill with a rope to pull himself on with every step, my son dropped to his knees and puked. He got up, took a few more steps, and puked again. This went on for 5 total pukings. I thought for sure he was done—he wasn't. Though he slowed down, he pushed on to the next obstacle up another hill about 200 yards away and kept going. I've never been more proud of puking in my life.

I don't know if he'll do this race again next year, but I don't care. What I do know is that he knows he can get knocked down, eat the ground, puke five times, then #GetUp and still go for another 45 minutes to finish a race. If he had quit after the puking, I would have totally understood. I don't know who said it, but one of my favorite quotes applies here to my son. I once read, "Anyone can give up, it's the easiest thing in the world to do. But to hold it together when everyone else would understand if you fell apart, that's true strength."

Getting knocked down is normal. Resting for a bit when we are down is normal. Sometimes we're not ready to #GetUp immediately. Sometimes, we need to eat some therapy ice cream or listen to a sad slow song on repeat for several hours straight. But putting an end to being down or helping loved ones put an end to being down, doesn't have to happen with a huge leap. One small move of slowly bringing one knee up to push off the ground and start climbing to our feet is all it takes for us to join the winners and #GetUp.

Chapter 11: Hating Happy

"Misery loves company" works in both a push and a pull manner. When we are miserable, we push others to become miserable with us. We want miserable company, we seek it out, we criticize and hate happiness because it makes us feel less alone. When others are miserable, we are very susceptible to getting pulled into their mindset. Maybe we allow ourselves to get pulled in because we just want our friend or family to feel less alone. And sometimes we get pulled into the misery train because we find a commonality and seize the opportunity to bitch to an attentive ear.

It's really easy to resist happiness when things aren't going well because human nature sends us down the path of least resistance. Reversing the momentum of the Struggle Bus is difficult. Staying where we are is not as difficult as breaking the cycle of struggling, even though we know what is better for us in the long run.

Combatting the dark spiral of misery is necessary for climbing toward light. Awareness is key. The more aware we are of the darkness of misery, the more able we are to #GetUp and deal with it. No light will flip on like a flashlight in the night. Things will slowly get less dark until it starts to feel less like dark and more like light at the end of a tunnel.

When our friends and loved ones are going through misery, we shouldn't feel bad about being happy and sharing that with them. So often I find myself comforting misery with misery because I don't want my struggling friend to feel isolated. But what our loved ones, or even we ourselves, really need during struggles is someone else to shed some light to help ignite a new flame. If we invite people into our happiness, we give them a path that they may be looking for. They may not accept our invitation right away, or ever, but the more paths people have to #GetUp on, the more likely we are to #GetUp sooner rather than later.

The gravity of failure and struggle gets heavier by the second. In my mid-30's, when I really dove deep into the racing life, "66%" was my arch nemesis. It was the worst part of anything I did. Grinding ain't easy, whether it's a short term grind, like a single race or a long term grind, like a six-month training program. For me, the grind was the darkest when I was 66% of the way in. Body parts hurt, sleeping is difficult, waking up is even more difficult, taking another step becomes infinitely harder after each previous step. Having finished 2/3 of something but knowing you still have another 33% left is daunting. I cannot count how many times I've uttered "this is the last (seven-letter adjective) time I'm ever doing this" around the 2/3 mark of a race.

However, recognizing this as my darkest hour has enabled me to work through it because I've chosen to embrace "happy" instead of hating it. Racing makes me happy; otherwise I wouldn't do it. I've had the most absurd "Why are you doing this?" conversations with myself before clicking the "Register" button online for almost every race I've done. The result of every one of those conversations is, "Because you enjoy it more than you hate it."

Everything we choose to do is just that, a CHOICE to do it. This doesn't only apply to racing and physical challenges. Jobs, relationships, family gatherings, and everything else in life all bring their own forms of darkness and misery. I'm not always right about my choices, but there is always something about every choice that I enjoy. When the misery sets in and I need to find a way to #GetUp and get through it, I find the "happy" that drove me to that decision. I grab onto that happy, I zoom in with full focus on that happy until I start to see the light. I may never do it again, but it gets me through the present.

When our friends and loved ones are seeking company for their misery, let's not join them. Instead, help them find and embrace the happy, instead of hating the happy. If we can love the happy, we can more easily face the darkness and #GetUp.

Chapter 12: Crevier... C-R-E-V-I-E-R... 9/29/39

My dad was my best friend. Though he never stood up in front of a classroom, he was a lifelong teacher. He taught me more than any traditional teacher has ever come close to teaching me. In primarily unconventional ways, he taught me everything from work ethic to math. He taught me how to shoot a gun, crack peanuts perfectly every time, fit enormous potato chips in my mouth without breaking them, and even how to take a nap in church while making it look like you're praying.

My dad was in the military for 24 years and was not only a perfect example of a lifelong learner, but also turned everyone he encountered into learners. I wasn't the only one he taught. He was constantly teaching everyone. Sometimes, he felt a little too strongly about the need to teach other people how to change lanes with the use of his middle finger, but teaching was in his blood. The most important thing he ever taught me was a lifelong lesson on how to live the #GetUp lifestyle and I am excited, honored, and humbled to be able to be sharing with you a piece of the household in which I was lucky enough to grow up.

When we're young, a lot of things go in one ear and out the other. But some things just stick with no rhyme or reason why. When I was 10 and my dad was teaching me how to play chess, I remember him telling me that the most important thing about chess was not to panic when put in check. He explained that most people immediately find the safest spot in which to hide and then they go hide there. "But," he said, "the move of winners is to counterattack." He explained the importance of first looking to see if there was a way to get out of check while putting the other person in check in the same move.

Life puts us in check so much and it's always so tempting to just shut down and go find a place to hide. I feel like I'm put in check damn near every day, in one way or another. But I was lucky enough to be coached by my father, at a young age, to always prioritize finding a way to stay on the offensive. One of my favorite thinkers, tweeters, and podcasters is Gary Vaynerchuck. His language is crass, but his messages have no fluff, and his content is loaded with things from which we can all learn. In one of his podcasts, he said, "When you are on the offensive, you smother excuses." I love that quote and it immediately made me think of my dad when I heard it. In addition to my dad's military-based love for offense, he could sniff out an excuse from a mile away. Whenever I would drop the ball on something and begin to "explain why", he would often ask me, "Is this a reason or an excuse?" I hate hearing excuses, and the worst is when I hear them come out of my own mouth. In order to #GetUp, we must first smother our excuses and decide to own the situation moving forward. It's not easy, but it's necessary.

We lost my dad, my best friend, six months ago to an 18-month battle with cancer. In the summer of 2016, he was diagnosed with Multiple Myeloma, an incurable cancer. I'm not going to pretend like our family suffered through anything special because cancer has impacted everyone in one way or another, and I know that millions of people have had worse battles than my father did. But what I feel does make us special is that we got to learn so much from him during his final year and a half of life.

I had a lot of time to mourn, before he even passed. I knew the reality of his situation and never really denied it. But I was still afraid of it. I was afraid of losing my dad. I was afraid of not having him around to help me #GetUp. I was afraid of not having him to call when I didn't know what to do about something. What's crazy is that I'm not missing my Dad. What he taught me has left me not needing him for those things. But what I didn't anticipate was how much I would miss my best friend. I didn't realize how much I would miss texting him when I found a great deal on something at Menards. I didn't realize how much I would miss calling him to talk about the Packers picking up Jimmy Graham in the off season. I didn't realize how much I would miss him making fun of me in a way that only a friend can do. I was ready for life to change and leave me without my Dad. I wasn't ready for life to leave me without my best buddy.

When life changes on us, we can fight it and be miserable or acknowledge it and find ways to enjoy the new normal. I'm not claiming that my Dad didn't have bad days during his battle, because I know he absolutely did. But he also owned the journey, as sucky as it was. I was fortunate enough to work for a school that bent over backwards to accommodate my need to take my dad in for treatment every Wednesday afternoon for the final 4 months. The time I got to spend with him brought us some incredible bonding, but what I got to see and learn from him was amazing.

He embraced his new norm, especially as the end rapidly approached. Walking into the cancer clinic and watching my dad check in was always an emotional undertaking. But its special feel never got old and almost brought me to tears every single time. Our weekly visit would begin with a chipper "Stan is here!" from the front-desk girl as if he were Norm in Cheers. Then came his new normal of going through the three-step routine of saying his name "Crevier" then spelling it "C-R-E-

V-I-E-R" then giving his date of birth "9/29/39".
After getting called back into our room, he would
joke with, entertain, and teach the nurses and
doctors something, typically about the Navy or the
Green Bay Packers. And then we'd move on to the
next stop for him to receive his chemo treatment
where again he would give his name, spell it, and
give his birthdate again.

I saw him go through the "Crevier... C-R-E-V-I-E-
R... 9/29/39" routine over a hundred times.
Every single time I choked back the tears. I don't
know how the heck he did it with such strength
and ownership of the situation. But he never
complained about it. In a time where we
encouraged him to be selfish, he was busy
teaching us how to keep living even while you're
super-busy dying.

My love of sports came from, yup, my dad. And
late in the fourth quarter of his life, he was down
big time. Just getting his butt kicked. There was
NO WAY he was coming back to win that game.
But he showed our family how to keep playing to
win the next play, even when we know the game is
almost over. He embodied what it means to live in
the moment. Living the #GetUp life is not about
always winning. It's about always believing that
you can still win the next possession or the next
act or the next 2 minutes, no matter what the
total score may be. However bad things seem,
even in the very end, we learned the importance of

embracing the new norm to #GetUp for whatever is left in front of you.

Overtime / Encore

There is a baseball-ism that says, "Some play 'til the time runs out. We play 'til we find out who's better." There are a lot of sports that have overtime, but there's nothing like hearing a baseball announcer say "...and we get some free baseball" in a tie game at the end of the 9th. I've never understood ending in a tie—man, why even play the game? As a coach, I've always prepared my players to play more than the standard amount. I would build in practice days where we would go for an extra 15–30 minutes on top of the scheduled practice time and my players would not find out about it until the very end of the originally scheduled time.

Being able and ready to "go more" than anticipated is an amazing asset. Digging deep when you "should be done" not only gives us an advantage, but it also gives our world an advantage over its previous situation. Everyone involved with the overtime or the encore benefits—not just the performer. Everyone gets more. Other than the opening song, I've never seen more energy from the crowd at a concert than when the band comes back out to the chants of "One more song!"

When I was a young kid, my uncle Gary had a four-wheeler. My dad, some of my cousins, his brothers, and I were getting ready to head up to their cabin in northern Wisconsin. I asked my Uncle Gary if he was going to be able to bring his four-wheeler up (like any 10-year-old boy would excitedly ask). He told me that he didn't think he'd have enough time to get it ready to bring up while he stopped at home before meeting us there. I completely understood but was super disappointed. A couple hours later, he arrived at the cabin... WITH the four-wheeler. Holy cow, was I pumped!! As we were riding it, I thanked him and questioned why he told me what he told me, but then ended up bringing it. He explained that he never wants to set someone up for disappointment and then said, "It's much better to over-deliver than to over-promise." This has stuck with me my whole life. So, in the spirit of that, here is a little more for you to take away from this word-filled event for which you bought a ticket.

You may have gotten to points along the way where you've read something and thought, "that's great and all, but HOW do I do that?" There's a reason that the phrase "actions speak louder than words" is such a popular phrase. If you have read this far, thank you! If you're reading this for yourself, for a loved one, or maybe even with a loved one, you are clearly committed to giving the #GetUp life a try. So here are a couple concrete action items that I've found will help start or re-energize the #GetUp way of living. I still come back to these when I need a #GetUp living booster shot because even I fade away from full commitment at times.

You don't have to do all of these. Remember, getting started only requires one small step. Just pick the one that seems most tolerable and find a way to try it out with a baby step. If you need some motivation, just jam some Pink—any Pink song will do. I have this crazy dream list in my head about being able to choose a couple celebrities to represent and endorse the #GetUp life and Pink is right there at the top of the list. So, welcome to the overtime/extra innings/ encore!

Chapter 13: No-Snooze Challenge

If you've read this far, I'm guessing it all sounds good and well to you. At the same time, I'm sure you may be wondering how to get started or how to help a friend or a family member or a student get started. Hopefully, by now, it's clear that I believe in baby steps. So, trying the no-snooze challenge (NSC) can be a great baby step for you or anyone else. The NSC is straightforward and something anyone can try because we all set alarms to wake up at some point.

Life is tiring. Life is like the honey badger and doesn't give a shit about anything. Sleeping is amazing, and I love it so much. It's the greatest escape from the insanity that life throws at us every day. I often catch myself daydreaming about how wonderful it's going to be that night to go to sleep. So, waking up for me is one of my greatest personal challenges, which I obviously battle on a daily basis.

Several years ago, I got so tired of hearing my alarm that it dawned on me I could minimize hearing that damn thing if I didn't snooze anymore. A great friend of mine has this uncanny ability to hear the alarm in the morning, immediately sit right up, put his feet on the floor, bound out of bed and function as if he's been awake for hours. Whenever I travel with him and share a hotel room, I'm always amazed and envious at the way with which he bounds into the day. So I thought I'd give it a try.

I first gave the NSC a try on a Saturday morning when I didn't have to go into work. I set my alarm for 30 minutes later than normal because if I wasn't snoozing, I could sleep an extra 30 minutes and still get out of bed at the same time. This math blew my mind, by the way, once I landed on that. When it went off in the morning, I was super mad as usual. But I knew I had to get up. So, I got up. I didn't hit snooze and I didn't even turn my alarm off until my feet were out from the covers and my torso was perpendicular to the floor. It was painful.

I did it again the next day, again without having to go to work. But I knew Day Three, Monday, was going to be my true test. So with a couple days of low-pressure practice, I set the alarm Sunday night for 30 minutes later than my standard Monday morning wake-up alarm. When it went off Monday morning, it wasn't easy, but it was doable. Very slowly, I rolled toward the edge of my bed, let my feet hit the floor, propped my torso upright, and turned off my alarm. I found new ways to swear during my 10-second trek into the bathroom to turn on the shower. It wasn't easy, but it didn't kill me. Little by little, day by day, it got easier (it's still not easy, just easier) for me to be a non-snoozer.

This is clearly not about waking up, but more about defeating procrastination. Building the mental strength to be able to do things right away also builds our ability to decide to bounce back from knockdowns and #GetUp.

Chapter 14: One More Time

Doing what's expected is good. Doing what's expected is necessary. Doing more than what's expected is where we can separate ourselves from what we are and what we actually can become. Sometimes we have circumstances come up where we do less than expected—that's natural. Sometimes those circumstances aren't great, like dealing with some sort of accident or emergency that takes priority (true priority, not a convenient excuse item) over what we're in the middle of accomplishing. Other times, those circumstances are fantastic, like winning by the 10-run rule in baseball and ending the game an inning or two before its normal length.

The "One More Time" (OMT) technique is measurable by nature. You may be going out for a three-mile run and at the VERY end (not saving up during the run to prepare for it) decide to keep running for one more block. Do not even think about this before or during any point in the run. For full effectiveness, OMT cannot be planned. It must occur at the very end of the original plan, no matter how empty our energy tank might feel.

Implementing OMT is not limited to physical activity. OMT at work could be as simple as "finishing" your 5:00 p.m. workday, looking at your personal calendar to see an empty evening ahead, and staying for another hour to get more work done. As a teacher, I absolutely hate grading (most do). For me, my OMT at work typically comes when grading projects or exams. If I plan to grade 10 items while I eat lunch, then maybe I finish that 10th one and OMT it by grading an 11th, even though I feel like my eyes are going to pop out of my head.

On the home front, there seem to always be a hundred things on the "to do" list. Working with our kids to raise them as #GetUp people, there is no better way than to model it. We can very easily find a chore to do WITH our children. Be intentional about choosing that chore so it can be turned into an OMT opportunity. By doing this, we as parents will be modeling and setting our children up to practice OMT. The more we, or our loved ones, practice OMT, the more ready we'll be when we are called on to #GetUp for more.

If you are working with a group of kids, or just within your own family, set up an "OMT Challenge." Create a weekly or monthly time frame during which you award points for each time someone finishes something, and then goes OMT with it. You can take these points and use them as currency to "buy" a later bed time for one night, or an ice cream treat, or anything else that's important to your group or family.

Remember to emphasize the criteria that it does not count as OMT if it's planned for before, or even during the regular length of the activity. If a person's chore is to cut the grass, and halfway through they decide they will edge and trim also, that's not a true OMT.

This type of challenge will also teach honesty and integrity during the self-reporting process. Only the person reporting will truly know if it was a genuine OMT, or if they cheated themselves by "saving up" energy. If it's not a struggle to dig deeper for OMT, then it's not truly building a stronger ability to #GetUp.

Chapter 15: Do It The Hard Way

Convenience is everywhere. Amazon Prime two-day shipping is one of the greatest conveniences in my life right now. I remember growing up without things like a microwave or call waiting. I don't think kids today even know what a busy signal sounds like on a phone. It's not their fault; it's just how it goes. For years before TV remote controls were even a thing, my dad had a TV remote control—me. I would stand up at the TV and change the channels for him until he was ready to commit to watching something. That was fun!

When we have to do without a convenience, it's comical to listen to each other complain about it. Then, inevitably someone caps off the ridiculous complaining by saying "#FirstWorldProblems" and we all laugh and move on. However, getting knocked down often involves losing some sort of convenience. Everything is relative, so losing something we are used to having creates a legitimate challenge, no matter how big or small. Think about the last time your internet was down—how disruptive was that? How did you respond?

I enjoy reading those "10 ways to..." lists. Some are cheesy, and some are serious, but they all get the juices flowing in my brain one way or another. Recently I read one that was about getting back to basics and slowing down your life. "Wonder without googling" was the one item on that list that really jumped out at me. We've become so programmed to "look it up" as soon as we wonder about something. But wondering without googling has been a lot of fun lately.

One way to build the #GetUp mindset is to find something in your life that you can try to do the hard way. Maybe you try it just once and see how it goes? But ideally, I think having something in our lives that we always do the hard way can help keep us grounded and strong.

When I was a kid, we would go to my Grandma and Grandpa Crevier's house in Green Bay, WI, a couple times a year. They did a LOT of things "the hard way." My favorite thing in their house was a sign that Grandpa Crevier had hung up that said, "When you cut your own wood, it warms you twice." I absolutely loved that sign.

Cutting my own wood is how I've embraced doing something the hard way. All of my friends order cords of firewood to be delivered to their house each fall. They used to always bug me to go in on it with them. They've stopped bugging me because they know I'm all in on cutting down, chopping up, and splitting my own firewood.

There's something about the sawdust from the chainsaw, the sound of wood crackling as it splits apart into a perfect wedge for the fireplace. It's a pain in the butt to deal with from start to finish and I love it. And every time I'm dripping sweat, questioning why the heck I'm not just ordering this stuff like everyone else, I remember my grandfather's sign.

So, do something the hard way. Appreciate the real work behind one of the many conveniences we enjoy in today's world. If you are able to find something that has a personal connection, it will be easier to keep on going with it. You don't have to stick with the first thing you test out, but keep trying different things the hard way until you are able to look at one and commit to it longer term. If you can find a way to enjoy it while it sucks, you are on your way to building a solid foundation to #GetUp.

Post-Game / After Party

I hope you've had as good of a time reading this book as I have had writing it. Many times through this process I've wondered why I'm putting so many other things on the shelf to write this. I've questioned if this is truly worth it. But then I go back to my original reason for creating the Twitter account and giving the TED Talk. If this helps just one person decide to keep living and not make an early exit, then it's worth it to me.

I hope you're able to try at least one of these overtime action strategies. If you do, I would love to hear about how it goes! Jump on Twitter and hit up our @GetUpLiving account and join our community online. Use our account to tell your #GetUp story by tweeting and mentioning @GetUpLiving. I'll retweet and share your story with others. The more we know about each other, the less lonely we feel when we struggle.

About the Author

Born in Jacksonville, FL, Sean moved to northern Illinois at the age of four, where he was raised halfway between Chicago and Milwaukee and grew up riding the line between Illinois and Wisconsin. He went to Purdue University for his undergrad degree in business and earned his master's degree in Secondary Education from Roosevelt University a few years later. He started teaching business classes and coaching several sports (golf, basketball, baseball) at Vernon Hills H.S. in 2000, after leaving the technology consulting world.

He currently wears several hats at his high school; teaching business, working with other teachers as an instructional technology specialist, and coaching golf. Outside of the school, Sean is a blogger for *Tech & Learning* magazine. He also works on a national accounting education team (accountingpilot.com) as a consultant for the AICPA (American Institute of Certified Public Accountants), training teachers on implementing college accounting curriculum into their high school courses. Sean has given several educational keynotes, workshops, and a TED talk, is the co-founder of the monthly #BusEdu chat on

Twitter, and absolutely loves teaching and learning.

He is an outdoor enthusiast, worse golfer than he'd like to be, even worse triathlete, Midwest native, Purdue Boilermaker, diehard Packer fan, and currently lives in northern Illinois with his wife and two kids.